B Willia
hl, Xina M.,
harrell Williams : music industry
tar /
27.07

3 4028 09630 8763
HARRIS COUNTY PUBLIC LIBRARY

S0-EPX-554

WITHDRAWN

PHARRELL WILLIAMS
MUSIC INDUSTRY STAR

BY XINA M. UHL

Published by The Child's World®
1980 Lookout Drive • Mankato, MN 56003-1705
800-599-READ • www.childsworld.com

Photographs ©: Jordan Strauss/Invision/AP Images, cover, 1; Featureflash Photo Agency/Shutterstock Images, 5, 9; Kevork Djansezian/Getty Images Entertainment/Getty Images, 6; Casey Rodgers/Fuse/AP Images, 10; Tina Fineberg/AP Images, 13; Matt Sayles/AP Images, 14; Alex J. Berliner/ABImages/AP Images, 16; S. Bukley/Shutterstock Images, 18; Richard Shotwell/Invision/AP Images, 20

Copyright © 2018 by The Child's World®
All rights reserved. No part of this book may be reproduced or utilized in any form or by any means without written permission from the publisher.

ISBN 9781503819955
LCCN 2016960918

Printed in the United States of America
PA02335

ABOUT THE AUTHOR

Xina M. Uhl has authored more than 15 books, including biographies and books on history and technology. She lives in sunny Southern California, where she spends far too much time reading. When she is not writing, she enjoys traveling, taking photographs, and hiking with her dogs. Her blog features her travel adventures and latest fiction projects.

TABLE OF CONTENTS

FAST FACTS 4

Chapter 1
ON TOP OF THE WORLD 7

Chapter 2
DESTINY COMES CALLING 11

Chapter 3
IN THE SPOTLIGHT 15

Chapter 4
MAN OF MANY TALENTS 19

Think About It 21
Glossary 22
Source Notes 23
To Learn More 24
Index 24

FAST FACTS

Name
- Pharrell (fah-REL) Williams

Birthdate
- April 5, 1973

Birthplace
- Virginia Beach, Virginia

Nickname
- Skateboard P.

Fun Trivia
- The original version of *Tom and Jerry* is Pharrell's favorite cartoon.
- Pharrell named his son Rocket after songs by Elton John, Stevie Wonder, and Herbie Hancock.
- Pharrell once wrote a song in only five minutes. He wrote it on his cell phone.
- As a young man, he went to the same church as rapper DJ Timbaland.
- The word *happy* repeats 57 times in Pharrell's Grammy-winning song, "Happy."

Chapter 1

ON TOP OF THE WORLD

The announcer's voice boomed out, "And the Grammy goes to . . ."[1]

The audience held their breath. Pharrell Williams sat in the front row, wearing a gray suit with a gray bow tie. It was the 57th Annual Grammy Awards on February 8, 2015.

Pharrell was one of five stars up for the Best Pop **Solo** Performance award. He was **nominated** for his song, "Happy." He had **composed** it for the movie *Despicable Me 2*.

The announcer's voice rang out. "'Happy'—Pharrell Williams!"[2]

◀ **Pharrell Williams performs his hit song "Happy" at the 57th Annual Grammy Awards.**

"Happy" began to play, and the audience burst into applause. Pharrell sat in his chair, stunned. Then he rose. He kissed his wife, model and fashion designer Helen Lasichanh. He shook hands and hugged those around him. Then he walked up the stairs to the stage to accept the award.

Pharrell was born in Virginia Beach, Virginia. His father, Pharoah, was a handyman. His mother, Carolyn, was a teacher and school librarian. Pharrell has two younger brothers and two half brothers. His grandmother watched him a lot while his parents worked. She enjoyed drums. So she asked him one day, "Why don't you learn how to play the drums?"[3]

Because of his grandmother, Pharrell went to band camp in the summer before seventh grade. At first, the drums seemed confusing. But a teacher named Ralph Copley showed Pharrell how to play them.

Pharrell remembers all his music teachers. There was Mr. and Mrs. Warren, Mr. Edwards, and Mr. Sharps.

▲ **Pharrell and Chad Hugo at the 32nd Annual American Music Awards**

"My story is the average story," he said. "It was filled with special people."[4]

One more special person was another student named Chad Hugo. Pharrell didn't know it yet, but Chad would change his life.

Chapter 2

DESTINY COMES CALLING

The sign above the front door read: Old Donation Center for the Gifted and Talented. Pharrell had joined this arts program through his middle school. Some students studied dance or art. Others, like Pharrell, wanted to learn music. As he toured the classroom for the first time, he saw a familiar face. It was Chad Hugo, the saxophone player from band class.

"Dude," he said. "Beginning band. You're still in it. I'm still in it. That's crazy."[5] Pharrell and Chad soon became good friends. When Pharrell was seventeen, he and Chad formed a band called the Neptunes. Chad played the saxophone. Pharrell sang and played the drums.

◀ **Pharrell (right) and Chad Hugo (left) perform in the band N.E.R.D.**

Their music blended hip-hop, rock, and pop. Pharrell didn't do this on purpose. He had just listened to many kinds of music growing up. "The radio station I listened to would play Queen, then Michael [Jackson], then Stevie [Wonder], then Genesis, then Madonna," he explained.[6]

A **talent scout** heard the Neptunes perform at a high school talent show. That brought them into contact with music producer Teddy Riley. Riley wanted to work with musicians who had **unique** sounds. The Neptunes were the answer. Riley said, "Those guys were so ahead of their time. That's what the Neptunes were about. They represented the future."[7]

With Riley as a mentor, Pharrell learned the music business. While still in high school, he wrote a verse for a popular Wreckx-n-Effect song. Pharrell and Chad decided the Neptunes's sound was too weird for the time. Instead, they moved into producing and writing hip-hop. There, they **thrived**.

▲ **The Neptunes wrote songs for popular artists such as Justin Timberlake (right).**

In the late 1990s and early 2000s, the pop and rap music they produced flooded the **airwaves**. The Neptunes worked with huge artists. These included Mary J. Blige, Britney Spears, Nelly, Justin Timberlake, and Snoop Dogg.

Pharrell's success got him noticed by the music world. But he was not done yet.

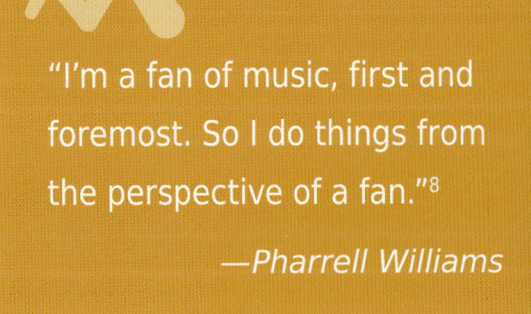

"I'm a fan of music, first and foremost. So I do things from the perspective of a fan."[8]

—Pharrell Williams

13

Chapter 3

IN THE SPOTLIGHT

Pharrell strode up to the camera. He clutched his leather jacket, under which he wore a striped shirt. Beaded bracelets and a flashy watch sat on his wrist. He wore gold rings on his fingers and a diamond earring. The magazine *GQ* was interviewing him about his fashion sense. "Style is wearing what you want to wear because it makes sense to you," he said. "It's the same thing in music. I do a lot of mixing and melding."[9]

Pharrell is known for his eye-catching style. In 2005, *Esquire* magazine named him the best dressed man in the world. It was easy to see why. He wore a mix of outfits from camouflage suits and tuxedos to shorts and leather jackets.

◀ **Pharrell's outfit for the 2004 *GQ* Men of the Year party**

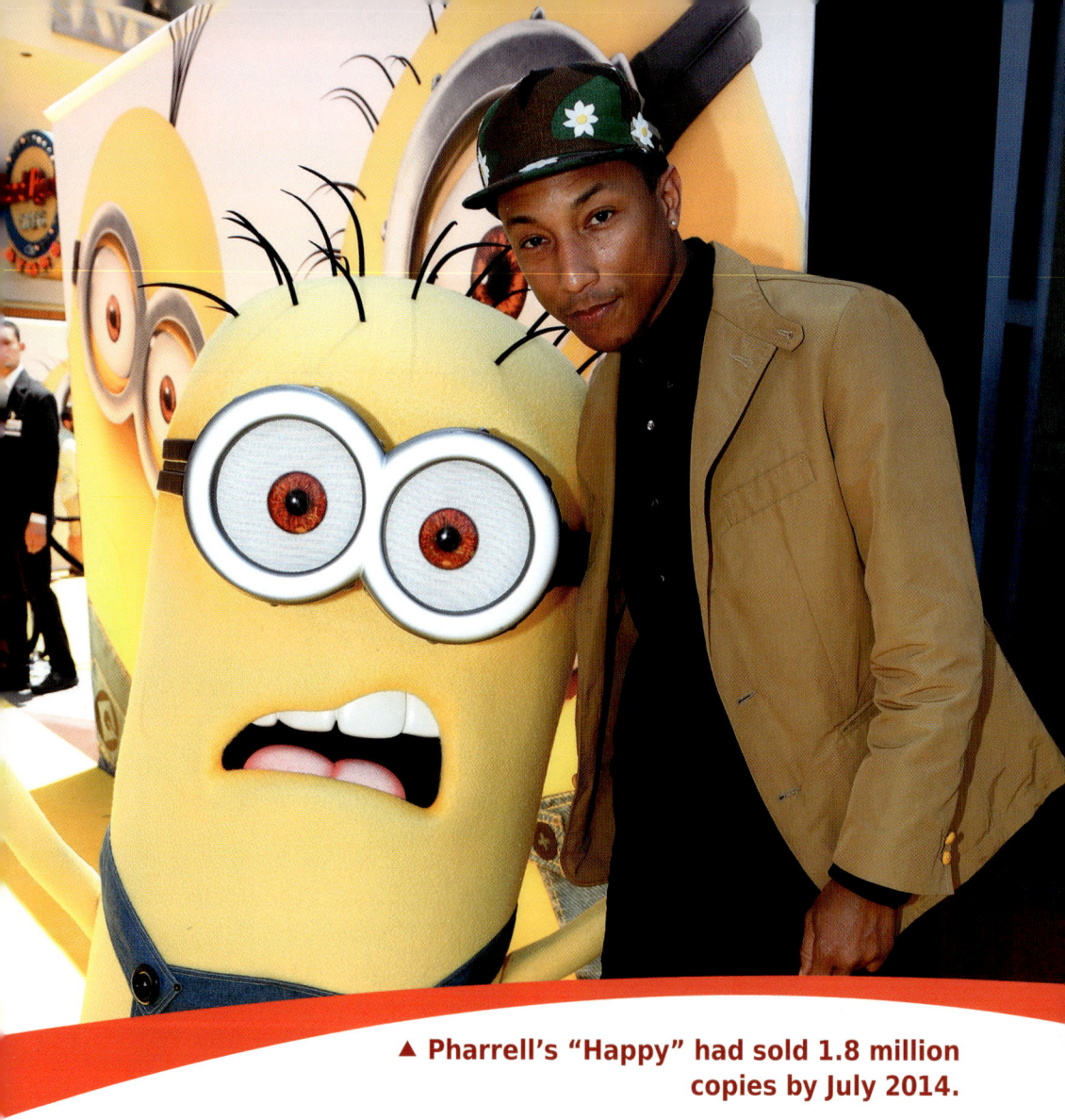

▲ Pharrell's "Happy" had sold 1.8 million copies by July 2014.

Pharrell showed off his style both in music videos and on stage. In 2001, Pharrell, Chad, and rapper Shay formed the band N.E.R.D. They put out four albums between 2002 and 2010.

Chad and Pharrell also formed record label Star Trak Entertainment in 2002. It represents N.E.R.D., singer-songwriter Robin Thicke, rapper Snoop Dogg, and others. Pharrell, a huge fan of the television show *Star Trek*, chose the record label name as a **play on words**.

> "My music is so much bigger than me, and what I am."[10]
>
> —Pharrell Williams, on the meaning of his music

Pharrell has also sung and danced with artists such as Jay-Z and Daft Punk. But he has not always teamed up with others. In 2006, he released a solo album, *In My Mind*. He wanted to make music his way, and he did that on this album. Another solo album, *G I R L*, came out in 2014. In between, he wrote the music for the 2010 film *Despicable Me* and its **sequel**.

Chapter 4

MAN OF MANY TALENTS

Skateboard wheels scraped along the concrete. Many skaters were enjoying the skate park, including Pharrell. "I'm always on the road, so I don't do it as much as I'd like," he said.[11]

He created a skate team called Icecream to help kids practice the sport. He also founded I Am Other. This company creates music, film, television, clothing, and more.

Pharrell has many interests. These extend to designing bikes and perfumes and making furniture and jewelry. He founded a charity called From One Hand to Another (FOHTA). FOHTA helps kids find their passions.

◀ **Pharrell wears a sweatshirt by his clothing design company, Billionaire Boys Club.**

▲ **Pharrell was a coach for the NBC television show, *The Voice*.**

It also donates school supplies and food to the needy and runs summer camps.

Music will always be Pharrell's number one interest. In 2013, he had a great year. He wrote three of the biggest songs, one of which was "Happy." He made music with many artists, including Daft Punk and Miley Cyrus.

Pharrell joined the television show *The Voice* from 2014 to 2016. He always pointed out each singer's positive traits, even when they were being eliminated from competition.

The 2016 film *Hidden Figures* used music written and performed by Pharrell. He helped compose the soundtrack and produce the film.

"To be a good person all my life until I die."[12]

—*Pharrell Williams, on his biggest goal*

One thing is certain about Pharrell. The future is wide open for this genius. As one of the busiest performers in the industry today, no one proves that more than he does.

THINK ABOUT IT

- How did Pharrell's partnership with Chad Hugo get him started in the music business?
- How did the music Pharrell listened to as a youth affect him?
- What do you think the future holds for Pharrell?

GLOSSARY

airwaves [AYR-wayvz]: Airwaves are signals that broadcast radio and television programs. Pharrell's song "Happy" was often on the airwaves.

composed [kum-POHZD]: When something is composed, it is created. Pharrell composed "Happy."

nominated [NAHM-ih-nayt-ed]: When someone is nominated, they are chosen for an honor. Pharrell has been nominated for many Grammy awards.

play on words [PLAY ON WERDZ]: A play on words means that the word or group of words has more than one meaning. Star Trak Entertainment is a play on words from the old *Star Trek* television show.

sequel [SEE-kwel]: A sequel is something that comes next. The animated movie *Despicable Me 2* is a sequel to *Despicable Me*.

solo [SOH-lo]: To do something solo is to do it alone. Pharrell has released several solo albums.

talent scout [TAL-ent SKOUT]: A talent scout looks for people who are good at a certain thing in order to convince them to work in a certain field. A talent scout put the Neptunes in contact with Teddy Riley.

thrived [THRYVD]: If something has thrived it has done well. The Neptunes thrived as a producer team.

unique [you-NEEK]: To be unique is to be one of a kind. The Neptunes had a unique music sound that producer Teddy Riley liked.

SOURCE NOTES

1. "Pharrell Williams Wins Best Pop Solo Performance." *The Grammys*. The Recording Academy, 8 Feb. 2015. Web. 13 Feb. 2017.

2. Ibid.

3. "Pharrell Williams: 'Happy' and Grateful." *CBS News*. CBS News, 13 Apr. 2014. Web. 13 Feb. 2017.

4. Ibid.

5. "Pharrell Williams on Meeting His Neptunes Partner Chad Hugo." *CBS News*. CBS News, 13 Apr. 2014. Web. 13 Feb. 2017.

6. Simon Hattenstone. "Pharrell Williams: 'My Music Is So Much Bigger than Me, and What I Am.'" *The Guardian*. The Guardian, 8 Mar. 2014. Web. 13 Feb. 2017.

7. Chris Williams. "Interview: Teddy Riley on His Virginia Years." *Red Bull Music Academy Daily*. Red Bull, 8 Apr. 2015. Web. 13 Feb. 2017.

8. "Interview with Pharrell Williams." *CNN*. Cable News Network, 20 Dec. 2013. Web. 13 Feb. 2017.

9. *GQ*. "Pharrell Shares His Style Philosophy – Style and How-To | GQ." *GQ* (blog), *YouTube*, 22 Jan. 2015. Web. 13 Feb. 2017.

10. Simon Hattenstone. "Pharrell Williams: 'My Music Is So Much Bigger than Me, and What I Am.'" *The Guardian*. The Guardian, 8 Mar. 2014. Web. 13 Feb. 2017.

11. John Arlidge. "My Sporting Life." *The Guardian*. The Guardian, 22 Nov. 2008. Web. 13 Feb. 2017.

12. Gavin Edwards. "Q&A: Pharrell Williams of N.E.R.D." *Rolling Stone*. Rolling Stone, 4 Jul. 2002. Web. 13 Feb. 2017.

TO LEARN MORE

Books
Flores, Christopher Lee. *Pharrell Williams*. New York, NY: Enslow Publishing, 2016.

Mattern, Joanne. *Pharrell Williams*. Hockessin, DE: Mitchell Lane Publishers, 2016.

Schwartz, Heather E. *Justin Timberlake: From Mouseketeer to Megastar*. Minneapolis, MN: Lerner Publications, 2015.

Web Sites
Visit our Web site for links about Pharrell Williams: childsworld.com/links

Note to Parents, Teachers, and Librarians: We routinely verify our Web links to make sure they are safe and active sites. So encourage your readers to check them out!

INDEX

Cyrus, Miley, 20

Daft Punk, 17, 20

Despicable Me (film series), 7, 17

family, 8

fashion, 15, 19

From One Hand to Another, 19–20

G I R L (album), 17

Grammy awards, 7

"Happy", 7–8, 20

Hidden Figures, 21

Hugo, Chad, 9, 11–12, 16–17

Lasichanh, Helen, 8

Neptunes, 11–13

N.E.R.D., 16–17

Star Trak Entertainment, 17

Voice, The, 20

Harris County Public Library, Houston, TX